The Bug Boys

by Celia Salerno
illustrated by Chi Chung

HOUGHTON MIFFLIN   BOSTON

Printed in China

ISBN 10: 0-618-88624-9
ISBN 13: 978-0-618-88624-1

89 0940 16 15 14 13
4500432004

Mark liked ants.
Gabe liked spiders.
Both liked bugs.
But they did not always agree.

2

"Look at all these ants," said Mark.

He had been trying to count them.

"I estimate there are 900 ants," he said.

"I'm going to put 235 in my ant farm."

Read • Think • Write If Mark takes 235 ants, how many ants will be left?

"Look at these four spider sacs," said Gabe.
"Each one holds about a hundred spider eggs.
"That is 400 eggs!" he said.

"I'm going to put 100 in my bug jar."

Read•Think•Write If Gabe takes 100 eggs, how many
eggs will be left?

4

"I will have 100 spiders," said Gabe.
"Spiders are silly," said Mark.
"They just lie around in their webs."
But as the eggs hatched, 18 spiders
crawled away.

Read • Think • Write How many spiders will Gabe
have now?

"Ants are too busy," said Gabe.
"They are all work and no play."
But the ants found a crack and 150 ants
crawled away.

Read • Think • Write How many ants does Mark
have now?

6

"My spiders!" said Gabe.

"My ants!" said Mark.

"Now we have zero bugs," they said together.

"It's better that they are free."

They both agreed.

Do You Feel Antsy?

Show

Read page 3. Draw one ant for each hundred ants.

Share

Question Read page 3. Talk about the total number of ants and the number of ants Mark is putting in his ant farm. How can you find the total number of ants left?

Write

Read page 3. Write a number sentence to show how many ants will be left after Mark takes 235 ants for his ant farm.